Elizabeth Fry

by L DU GARDE PEACH OBE MA PhD DLitt
with illustrations by ROGER HALL

Ladybird Books Ltd Loughborough

ELIZABETH FRY

Elizabeth Fry was born in Norfolk in the year 1780. Conditions in England then were very different from those of today. When, as a young woman, she went from place to place, preaching and visiting prisons, there were no railways: the horse was still the main means of transport and people travelled at a speed no greater than did the Romans.

Many aspects of life were no better than they had been hundreds of years earlier. As a child she had been taken to see a 'house of correction' in Norwich. It was a horrifying experience for a child from a rich, comfortable home and with kind and indulgent, if strict, parents. The memory of it never left her. When, later, she visited Newgate prison at the suggestion of a minister of the Society of Friends, as the Quakers were called, she was warned that the prisoners were vicious and dangerous. She found them infinitely pitiful.

The women prisoners were ragged and with no hope of better conditions. No-one cared what happened to them. But Elizabeth believed that God cared and that people like herself could help them.

So a life-time's work opened before this simple, Christian woman. Sincere in her belief in goodness, she was determined to help in what she believed to be God's work. Doubts often troubled her, but once she was certain that what she was doing was right, nothing was allowed to stand in her way. Mocked and scorned, she never forgot that Christ had been mocked and his disciples martyred for their belief. She felt that she must be as strong in her faith as they had been.

0 7214 0337 9

There are few, if any, of us living today who did not have one or more of our ancestors in prison during the last thousand years. Kings, presidents, princes, patriots and prime ministers, guilty or innocent, have at one time or another suddenly, and often unexpectedly, found themselves looking out from behind prison bars.

Sometimes the prisons were reasonably comfortable, depending upon the importance or wealth of the prisoner: more often they were not. In the days when it was possible to be imprisoned, and even executed for stealing an article worth a shilling, prison was likely to be a very uncomfortable place indeed. It was not meant to be anything else.

Anyone owing money was liable to be arrested and sent to a debtors' prison until the money was paid. It was often difficult, if not impossible, to obtain enough money to repay even a small debt. Some of the unfortunate debtors remained for months or even years in conditions unworthy of a civilised country.

In stories by authors such as Charles Dickens, we may read accounts of the shocking state of such prisons in London and elsewhere during the first half of the last century. Prisoners guilty of serious crimes often had iron rings fastened on their ankles and attached to a chain round their waists. These terrible 'irons' as they were called, were riveted together and the unhappy wrong-doer wore them, day and night, until he or she was released or died. Sometimes the chains were attached to an iron ring cemented into the wall, and it required a blacksmith to remove them.

Not all prisons were so bad. In about 1820 it was not as dreadful to be a prisoner in Manchester as it was in Carlisle: Edinburgh prisons were probably a little better than either of them. In York, wretched prisoners were heavily loaded with irons and were almost without clothing. In some prisons the inmates had to live, if they managed to survive at all, on less than two penny-worth of bread a day: in others they could eat an occasional meal of soup and beef and potatoes. It all depended on the governor of the prison.

In one thing the prisons of today still resemble those of the early years of the last century: they are all over-crowded. This is partly because there are more people living in the British Isles today, and also because there is always more crime in a country after a great war. When many thousands of men have been trained to use deadly weapons and encouraged to kill other men, they are not all likely to return peacefully to ordinary civil life.

We must also remember that when armies are demo-bilised, there are always thousands of men for whom there is no work. If crime is the only way to provide food for their families, men who are demobilised are well equipped for a career of violence.

In the year 1780 a daughter was born to a wealthy family in Norwich. She was christened Elizabeth and, when she grew up, she succeeded in changing the conditions in prisons in many of the countries of Western Europe.

Elizabeth's parents were John and Catherine Gurney and they belonged to the religious sect known as 'Quakers'. Elizabeth was one of twelve children, at a time when it was usual for people to have large families. They lived in the stately mansion of Earlham Hall, and for generations had been members of the 'Society of Friends'. John Gurney was a merchant and banker: he was successful because the Quakers were known and respected for honesty in all their dealings.

To say that a man is a Quaker does not mean today what it did in the days of Charles I. It was then an insulting name given to members of the Society of Friends because they were sneeringly accused of quaking with emotion at their religious gatherings. Although their correct name is still the Society of Friends, the name 'Quaker' has rightly become not only respectable but one which implies strict honesty and truthfulness.

From the time of Henry VIII there have been many sects which have broken away from the English Church. They were persecuted, but they continued to exist. Often they were obliged to meet in secret, in country houses, sheds and barns, and were always in danger of betrayal to the Church authorities.

If we are to understand why a rich, lively, and attractive girl like Elizabeth Gurney should wish to help the inmates of the prisons of her day, we must know something about George Fox and the other founders of the Society of Friends, and of what they believed and practised.

George Fox, born in 1624, was the son of a weaver in Leicestershire. He was appalled by the bitter religious hatreds of differing sects. On all sides he saw honest God-fearing men and women persecuted and imprisoned by others who also professed to be followers of Christ. He dreamed of a fellowship of those who had no strict creed or form of religious service, who recognised no priests or bishops and who freely allowed others to worship God in any way that seemed good to them. They wanted women to be judged as the equals of men before God, and to take part in the organisation of the Society, a thing unheard of before in England.

So George Fox and others became the founders of the Society of Friends, scornfully referred to as Quakers by those who disagreed with them. They lived simply and honestly; they dressed in sober garments when, in the reign of Charles II, men as well as women wore silks and satins and lace. They avoided the pleasures of music and dancing and to them the theatre was utterly wicked. They used an old form of speech, addressing each other always as 'thee'.

But above all, they were honest. They were persecuted for their religious beliefs, but trusted for their commercial honesty. They were not dreamers: they were practical, intelligent, and successful in their business dealings.

By the time Elizabeth Gurney was born, many Quakers had become much less narrow-minded: they no longer thought that music and dancing were necessarily wicked. Although her parents continued as good, sober-minded citizens, they did not prevent Elizabeth from visiting fashionable London, buying pretty clothes, and even going to the theatre to see 'Hamlet'. She took lessons in dancing and went to the Opera. For a short while she lived the same sort of life as any other gay, lively and attractive young girl who had enough money to buy whatever she wanted. Elizabeth was not yet twenty, and there is no doubt that she enjoyed life.

Most of the young people she met in London were quite content to enjoy the good things life offered. But not Elizabeth. She was a serious-minded girl. She compared the gay life of fashionable London society with the misery of the lives of the poor. Her home life and the example of her parents, made her feel that much was wrong in the world. She was anxious to do something about it: but what?

To give money to the poor was not enough. She felt that she had to do something more personal. When she was only eighteen she had been taken to hear a famous American preacher. She was so emotionally affected that, in the words of her sister, she wept most of the way home.

It was after this experience that she visited London. Elizabeth was already the sort of woman to decide things for herself. She was also fair-minded: she always examined both sides of a problem before making a decision.

Elizabeth Gurney was not a prig. When she wrote in her diary, "I have felt that there is a God", she meant it. She did not suddenly become a religious 'do-gooder'. Her belief was the result of deep thought and much inward questioning. She described her mind as "clothed with light, as with a garment". This was not written for effect. Unless we can understand her state of mind, we shall never understand Elizabeth Fry.

This is, of course, the name by which she became famous throughout Europe. In 1800 she married Joseph Fry, described as a rich London merchant and a member of a Quaker family which was strict in its refusal to enjoy many of what we would regard as the harmless pleasures of life.

To this Elizabeth made no objection. She had already adopted the sober dress of a Quaker. The simple, dark dress with its broad, white collar and white head-dress must have suited the pretty matron of twenty. The contrast with the low-necked, frilled and flowered, brilliantly coloured dresses of the young girls of the neighbourhood was no doubt very striking, but there is no suggestion that Elizabeth was dressing for effect. She continued to dress soberly, and often unfashionably, for the rest of her life.

Elizabeth Fry was utterly and completely sincere. She was ready to give up many things, such as singing, of which the more strict Quakers disapproved. In her diary she wrote "How much my natural heart does love to sing". She felt most truly that to be happy through singing, even when singing hymns, was wrong because it was an emotion which was independent of God.

From the time when Elizabeth first began to think about how the world might be made a better place for others, she came up against questions which must have seemed difficult to answer. One instance was her attitude to her servants. In those days people as wealthy as Joseph Fry were able to employ a number of servants. Elizabeth was not only anxious to save their souls, but also to treat them as fellow human beings. This was natural to the Quakers, who believed that one human soul was as good as another.

At the same time she was the mistress of her household, and it was part of her duty to insist that the servants did their various jobs honestly and conscientiously. She told them that in God's sight she and they were equal, but that they must still do their work properly.

The Quakers were determined to be free from many of the ordinary rules of society. It is told of Elizabeth's brother that, as a guest in the house of fashionable friends, he insisted on keeping his hat on. We can well imagine that he was not afterwards asked to many fashionable dinner parties.

A Quaker Meeting House is not regarded by the Quakers as a sacred place. For this reason, Quakers do not take off their hats when they enter it, as men do when they go into a church.

When she was nineteen, Elizabeth had had grave doubts as to whether it was better that she should marry, or devote herself entirely to the Quaker ideal of service to others. After she married Joseph Fry and although she had ten children, she was still able to make her influence felt all over Western Europe. In later years she did not let marriage interfere with her preaching.

Unlike the Church of England or the various non-conformist sects, the Quakers did not have priests who devoted all their time to the service of a congregation. Anyone who wished to do so was permitted to speak at a Quaker Meeting, women as well as men, though there were some, of course, who were better speakers than others and who were heard more often. Quakers regarded these as their 'ministers', but they met in silence and it was not unusual for this silence to continue until the congregation dispersed.

Elizabeth had received a good education at a time when only girls of wealthy families could get any sort of education worthy of the name. She was conscious of her ability, and had already spoken briefly in meetings. Eleven years after her marriage she was recognised as a 'minister' by the Society of Friends.

After marrying Joseph Fry she lived in London for nine years. In 1809 she and her growing family moved to a spacious mansion, Plashet House, in Essex. Here she lost the feeling of nervousness which made her shy and often silent; she was certain that she had a duty to speak words which, she believed, "God wanted to be heard".

The feeling so common among members of the Society of Friends, that wealth and opportunity were not to be selfishly enjoyed but must be used to help others, no doubt influenced Elizabeth Fry considerably. A wealthy woman who deliberately visited disease-ridden convicts in filthy gaols would today be 'news', but Elizabeth Fry was not looking for publicity. She deeply believed that she was doing God's work. Pity and her strong religious conviction impelled her to continue.

It was in 1813 that she first visited the prison known as Newgate. What she saw there made an impression upon her which she never forgot.

The young and happy wife and mother did not visit Newgate as an inquisitive tourist. Her thought was to bring gifts of food or clothing to those in prison, many of whom were suffering through no fault of their own. She found that gifts were not enough. Her instinct for ordinary, decent living was outraged by what she saw. She came away convinced that the whole prison was badly organised, badly run and without any regard for the decencies of life.

Whether Elizabeth decided there and then that something had to be done, and that she was the person to do it, we do not know. Her Quaker conscience was stirred and she returned to her comfortable home deeply troubled. During long hours of thought and prayer she sought for guidance from that 'Inner Light' which never failed her. It was not until four years later that she saw clearly what she must do.

Domestic duties and the care of a growing family had kept Elizabeth Fry fully occupied during the next four years. It was not until then that she returned to Newgate with time to devote to affairs other than those of her own household.

About Christmas, 1816, Elizabeth's brother-in-law, himself a Quaker, was very troubled by the problem of what to do with 'juvenile delinquents', boys and girls who were not yet criminals but might easily proceed from mischief to crime.

Elizabeth realised in full the importance and difficulty of the problems which were worrying her brother-in-law. But her concern was not only with juvenile delinquency: it included the whole of the prison system of those early years of the century. Prisoners were punished by solitary confinement in dark, underground dungeons; men, women and children were transported to Botany Bay in Australia in old, unseaworthy, and overcrowded wooden ships; they were heavily chained and often beaten by vindictive warders.

No complaints ever received attention; the word of the most brutal warder was always believed. Prisons were so full that the authorities were only too anxious to get rid of prisoners as quickly as possible.

In 1817, after another visit to Newgate, Elizabeth Fry really began her long struggle against the stupidity and obstinacy, the prejudice and inefficiency of the prison authorities. The prison authorities, stupid as they were, were not the only ones to blame for what she found. A man or woman went to prison because he or she had been arrested by the police, and tried in a Court of Law by a magistrate or a judge who, in the year 1817, could be and sometimes was, more stupid and ignorantly prejudiced than the police or the prison warders.

In one London prison Elizabeth found a boy of seventeen 'of very decent appearance' who had been sentenced to prison by a magistrate because his employer had accused him of idleness. It was very easy to get into prison in 1817, but almost impossible to get out.

Convicted persons were led to prison handcuffed to a chain. In the prisons over-crowding and underfeeding were common. In Wakefield, a prison built to hold 110 prisoners was found in 1817 to contain 1,602 men and 278 women. Magistrates complained that crime was increasing and that criminals had to be sent somewhere. There were simply not enough prisons.

What was largely to blame for many of the harsh sentences was the memory, still fresh in the minds of the upper classes, of the horrors of the French Revolution, when the French King had been murdered by the mob.

When a woman as determined and capable as Elizabeth Fry began to take an interest in anything, the authorities decided it was wise to pay attention to her reports. This was more especially so when the criticism came, not from some minor official or employee, but from a woman belonging to a wealthy family and who might have influential friends. All down the ages, paid officials have always been careful not to offend anyone who might be in a position to influence their own superiors: this fact has been the cause of bad government ever since the days of the Roman Empire: it is not unknown today.

Elizabeth did not have influential friends, but she had courage and determination. Even more important in the days of the religious revival of the early nineteenth century, she was intensely religious. Nervous officials knew that to offend against religion was more dangerous to their positions than anything else.

Elizabeth Fry believed utterly and sincerely that God had called her to the task of reforming the prisons of her day. Anyone who attempted to prevent her was, in her view, the enemy of God. It was as simple as that.

Not that her task was easy. There were many men, from the Home Secretary down to the warders in the prisons, who resented any interference, especially from a woman. There were many ways in which they might make it more difficult for her even to *see* the prisoners. Elizabeth Fry did not argue. When the Governor of a prison was trying to put difficulties in her way, she simply looked at him. Soon he would begin to shuffle uneasily. God had won.

The year 1817 was not a very hopeful year for prison reform. Everywhere there were troubles, of one sort or another, which frightened the governments of western European countries. There was much poverty and hunger among the working class in Britain, and their distress made them desperate.

The price of corn made bread too dear for poor people to buy, and mobs of hungry men and women rioted against the Government. In Spar-fields they tried to seize the Tower of London, and in Derby a mob had to be dispersed by the army. In Manchester there was the 'Peterloo' riot, where a gathering of many thousands of workmen was charged by the Yeomanry. All these caused grave concern to the Government.

The system of 'enclosures', by which common land was taken over by rich men, meant that poor men had nowhere to pasture their pigs or even a single cow, if they had one. Nor had they anywhere to grow vegetables. They were obliged to work for the rich at a miserable wage on land which had once been free for them to use. At the same time the invention of machinery for weaving replaced the hand-looms in the cottages, and more and more poor people found themselves without work.

Because of the widespread protests, an act, called by the Latin name 'Habeas Corpus', which says that a person must be brought to trial and not be held indefinitely in prison, was suspended. Many innocent people, guilty only of protesting against poverty and starvation, were arrested and put in prison without a chance to prove their innocence.

It seemed that only by crime could a poor man hope to feed his wife and family. Poaching was common, and fierce fighting took place between gangs of desperate poachers and gamekeepers. Many poachers were killed or injured: others were caught in iron man-traps which closed on their feet and legs with savage saw-edged, metal jaws worked by powerful springs.

It was a terrible time for the poor. Out-of-work farm-labourers were sometimes gathered into small groups by overseers and auctioned to any man prepared to bid for their labour. They were the lucky ones: the others starved.

So the prisons were filled and over-filled. Brutal and ignorant men were often recruited as warders or even governors. Here is a prison notice which shows how low was the standard of education of those in charge. It was pasted on the wall of the so-called common-room of one of His Majesty's prisons:

> The Rules of this Room for every man that come
> in this to pay 3d for Cols Sticks and Candels.
> When you fust com in Tow Men to Clen this
> Room and the youngest Prisener to do anything
> that is arsk.
> Any one
> that is cort polan this down will
> have three donson.

When six Dorset labourers met together to form a trade union, and were arrested and sentenced to transportation to Tasmania, public opinion forced the Government to pardon them. They were actually arrested for promising to keep their meetings secret, which was illegal. The six men were not criminals. All were honest men: one of them a Methodist preacher.

Elizabeth Fry began her work by finding out how women prisoners were treated. Together with other members of the Society of Friends she formed an 'Association for the Improvement of the Female Prisoners in Newgate'. One of the aims of the Association was to bring to the prisoners a knowledge of the Bible.

The Quakers had great faith in the Bible as a means of turning criminals from their evil ways. Elizabeth Fry gathered the women prisoners together and read the Bible to them. The women made no objection. But soon Elizabeth, who was a very practical woman, realised that this was not enough. The prisoners needed better food, they needed clothing and better accommodation. Above all, they needed something useful to do, and instruction in how to do it.

Elizabeth Fry believed that if men and women became criminals, they were not so much to blame as the conditions of the times in which they lived. She was certain that if so-called criminals were treated as human beings they would become better men and women.

It was when the practical side of her nature became active that she was able to exert the influence which did so much to change prison life for men and women alike. When she said that she, and the respectable and wealthy Quaker women of the Association, were ready to mix with the prisoners, she and they meant it. Some of the prisoners resented it at first, but the obvious honesty of the Quakers overcame their resentment.

NOTICE is hereby given, That should any of the Bibles Prayer Books or other Printed Books which are deposited in the ward for the use of Prisoners be mutilated or defaced, every prisoner in the Ward where such offence may occur, will be held responsible and be subject to such punishment as the Keeper may direct.

The Quaker women of the Association drew up a set of rules. Of these the most important were: (1) That a matron be appointed for the general superintendence of the women, and (2) That the women be engaged in needlework, knitting, or any other suitable employment. Today such employment for women prisoners may sound old-fashioned, but it was a great improvement on the previous idleness and boredom.

Punishment was forbidden, except for short periods of solitary confinement for serious offences. The fact that it was Elizabeth Fry who persuaded the Home Secretary to agree to such a rule made the prisoners look upon her as a woman of real influence and sympathy on their behalf. Most important of all was that she was working on their behalf from her experience of conditions inside the prisons, not just making senseless rules from outside.

Elizabeth Fry became a public figure. She was recognised as an authority on prison reform, and no prison governor in Great Britain dared refuse to admit her on a visit of inspection. Everywhere she preached that 'Kindness is better than chains'.

In the early years of the century many women were transported in the infamous convict-ships to the other side of the world. So long as they were in British prisons, Elizabeth Fry could help them: the moment the ship sailed, they were beyond her help. During the long voyage in an over-crowded ship it was easy for them to forget all that she had taught them. On a ship the captain, out of touch with land for weeks at a time, was all-powerful.

Two years after the formation of the Association, a book was published of which Elizabeth Fry and her brother, Joseph, were joint authors. This was a diary of what they had found during a tour of the prisons of Scotland. The book was praised by the Government, and led to official improvements in English as well as Scottish prisons. It was also read abroad and led to many invitations to visit prisons all over Europe.

The year following the publication of the diary another wealthy and equally public-spirited woman was born. Her name was Florence Nightingale, about whose work you may read in another book in this series. It is not too much to suggest that conditions in prisons and hospitals might be very different today, had it not been for their devoted work. At a time when women were expected to be content to be wives and mothers and not to interfere in public affairs, it demanded courage and determination, as well as the ability to fight prejudice and masculine narrow-mindedness, to do what these two women did.

Florence Nightingale is the better known of the two, though her period of active influence was short. She caught the imagination of the public in a way that Elizabeth Fry neither sought nor achieved. Both were regarded by those in immediate authority as interfering busybodies.

Now began for Elizabeth Fry a period of much travelling and intense activity. Italy, France, Denmark and Holland, Belgium, Switzerland and Russia were all interested to learn about her work in prison reform. She was very willing to share her knowledge and experience with them.

In November, 1828, misfortune overtook Elizabeth Fry and her family. Her husband became bankrupt and they were no longer able to remain in their large house. For a time Elizabeth was very unhappy. They were not poor and were still able to live well and comfortably. But Elizabeth was troubled by the thought that their misfortune was God's punishment for something which she had done or left undone.

The new status of the family affected her work. What had to be regarded as important when done by the rich Elizabeth Fry, was not necessarily to be tolerated from the poor Mrs. Fry. She was obliged to ask for help from her wealthy friends to finance the charities which she had previously supported out of her husband's income. She felt that she was no longer listened to as an authority.

A committee on prisons and the punishment of criminals held that her views on prison reform were not practical. Her belief that if criminals were treated kindly, God would turn their thoughts from further crime, was openly mocked in the House of Commons. The prison inspectors believed in punishment, the more painful the better. They proved their case by selecting the most hardened and vicious criminals as examples of those who could not be changed by kindness.

It was thought to be very clever when someone said that "women knitting in Newgate had as much influence on prison reform as the burning of the cakes by King Alfred had upon English cooking". In fact, Elizabeth Fry was looked on as an emotional woman, easily imposed upon by any criminals who pretended to be religious.

One of the improvements carried out by the Association had been the setting up of a shop inside the prison. This was known as Mrs. Brown's Shop, at which prisoners were able to buy such things as tea or coffee, sugar and butter. The new official prison inspectors were very much against it. They supplied the prisoners with a quart of gruel and one pound of bread a day, with a small amount of meat or soup on alternate days, and a pound of potatoes a week. To permit them to buy such luxuries as tea or coffee, was to make a prison so attractive that many women would commit a crime to get into it.

They said that tea and coffee were for honest people, and if criminals desired such things all they had to do was to remain honest. The Quakers on the committee of the Association, though themselves good religious women as the inspectors admitted, were regarded as too 'soft' in dealing with hardened criminals. They denounced Mrs. Brown's quite harmless shop as being, in the words of their report, "productive of much evil".

Food had always been smuggled into Newgate. Many of the warders were making money by supplying, as Elizabeth Fry pointed out, chicken and wine to those who could afford it. This was a way of making money which the warders were unwilling to give up, and the governor—whether he had any share in it or not—considered it better not to interfere.

It was obviously quite impossible to make any arrangement which would satisfy both Elizabeth Fry and the prison officials.

As Elizabeth Fry grew older, a strange thing happened. She became a legend in her own lifetime. Much of her work on behalf of female prisoners had been undone by a new generation of prison inspectors; the Government had no sympathy with reformers. But Elizabeth Fry was by now firmly fixed in the minds of ordinary people as a very good and religious woman who was kind to those less fortunate than herself. She may have been wrong, they said, but she meant well.

Largely defeated as a prison reformer, she became a personality socially. When the King of Prussia visited England, she entertained him at her house in London. Although Elizabeth Fry as a good Quaker, held all human souls as of equal value, she was always flattered by the attentions of royalty. To entertain a King was for her one of the great occasions of her life. She would have been surprised to know that her name and her work would be remembered and honoured by many people long after that of Frederick William IV, King of Prussia, was forgotten.

On another occasion she was entertained by the Lord Mayor of London at the Mansion House. This was in recognition of her life's work on prison reform.

As Elizabeth Fry took her seat between the Prince Consort, the husband of Queen Victoria, and Robert Peel, Prime Minister of England, she had come a long way from the visit to Newgate in 1813.

Elizabeth Fry believed that if more people were able to read and write, there would be less crime. Amongst the women prisoners in Newgate, one in every three could not read at all, and another third were only able to read words of one syllable. Few of them were able to write. This seems very strange to us, when children of eight or nine read this book without difficulty, except for some of the longer words.

Even those prisoners who had learnt to read, had forgotten how to write. Poor people did not write letters. What was the use, they said, when so few of their friends or relations could read? It was quite common for some person who could read and write to charge a few pence for writing or reading letters for others in a village. Even today there are four or five grown up men and women in every hundred who are what we call illiterate: that is, they are unable to read or write.

Attached to every prison was a chaplain. He preached on Sunday in the prison chapel, and he was in charge of any education given to the prisoners. But many of the chaplains thought that it was a great mistake to teach the poor to read. It was, they said, the writers in France who had been responsible for the French Revolution.

Some of the younger women prisoners were obliged to bring their children into prison with them; it was with these children that Elizabeth Fry made a start in the teaching of reading.

Many of the prison authorities thought that Elizabeth Fry expected too much from religious instruction. They mocked secretly at her reading from the Bible to women who understood little and cared less. They even accused her of 'showing off' before the friends whom she invited to these meetings.

That this was not true is shown by the many other activities in which she took part or which she started. Real distress always won her sympathy. In Brighton she, and a visiting Society which she organised, managed to ensure that such help as was available went to those who were destitute through no fault of their own. Those who made a trade of begging were shown up for what they were.

It is difficult for us to understand the point of view of those who, until well into the last century, found unfortunate lunatics amusing. These people would go to a sort of hospital known as Bedlam, to laugh at the queer antics of the insane. It was considered a pleasant afternoon's amusement, similar to a visit to the zoo. Sympathy with the unfortunate was not one of the kindly virtues in 1800.

Elizabeth Fry was different. Her Quaker upbringing and her instinctive feeling for the troubles and unhappiness of others, made her deeply sympathetic towards the mad men and women shut up in Bedlam. The hospital attendants made a living out of charging people to come in, which further roused the indignation of Elizabeth Fry. Her energy and determination changed conditions for the better.

We should always be thankful for the work of a woman like Elizabeth Fry. She was one of the great women of the nineteenth century. She never spared herself when she could be of help to others. Her work in prisons was to her a proof that God cared for the unhappy and the unfortunate.

Her reputation as a prison reformer quickly spread over Europe. Whenever possible she answered all calls for advice and help. Only a month before she was taken seriously ill, she went to Paris at the invitation of the French Government. Her only reward was the gratitude and love of those whom she had helped.

Though often ignored by the stupid politicians of her day, she was loved by many poor and unhappy men and women. Politicians are forgotten: she is remembered.

There have been many prison reformers since her time. Some have done much good. The prisons of previous centuries were dirty, insanitary, and often in the charge of brutal governors and warders. No-one cared what became of the prisoners, once they were safely under lock and key. Some had never been tried by a jury, as was their right; some were innocent; some were hardened criminals. Elizabeth Fry, a good and brave woman, devoted her life to trying to reform wrong-doers, instead of punishing them.

Series 561